Skills for Young Writers

Written by
Rhonda Chapman

Cover Illustration
by
Vickie Lane

Publishers
Instructional Fair • TS Denison
Grand Rapids, Michigan 49544

Permission to Reproduce

Credits

Authors: Rhonda Chapman
Cover Artist: Vickie Lane
Project Director: Rhonda DeWaard
Editors: Elizabeth Flikkema, Linda Kimble, Sharon Kirkwood
Production/Layout: Pat Geasler

Standard Book Number: 1-56822-587-3
Skills for Young Writers–6
Copyright © 1997 by Instructional Fair • TS Denison
2400 Turner Avenue NW
Grand Rapids, Michigan 49544

Table of Contents

Introduction

Skills for Young Writers is a reproducible book designed to turn novice writers into fluent writers. These high-interest grade-appropriate lessons can be used to enhance and strengthen proofreading and revising skills.

This book contains fiction and nonfiction selections which focus on various skills such as grammar, punctuation, and spelling. Suggested Revisions/Extensions at the end of each lesson provide additional activities that may be considered for expanding writing skills.

The lessons are designed to be used as teaching transparencies and student worksheets. There is ample space on each page to allow for corrections. In some cases, revisions or extensions may require a separate sheet of paper. The Answer Keys at the back of the book may be used as a guide for the teacher, although students may include additional revisions. Skills taught in these lessons may be reinforced in students' personal writing.

About the Author

Rhonda Chapman has eight years of classroom experience. She received her undergraduate degree from Grand Valley State University where she majored in special education. Rhonda also holds a Masters of Education Degree, along with a reading endorsement, from Grand Valley State University. She enjoys assisting home school families and does a great deal of private tutoring.

Steps for Successful Writing

Prewriting

- Brainstorm topics you might like to write about.

- Create a list of things you could write about each topic.

- Choose the topic you know the most about and that would be of interest to others.

- Collect information.

- Consider your audience and purpose for writing.

Writing

- Write a rough draft focusing on what you want to say rather than the spelling and mechanics.

- Skip every other line when writing your rough draft to leave space for corrections.

Revising

- Read your draft, making changes for interest and clarity.

- Ask another person to listen to your writing and to offer suggestions for improvement.

Editing and Proofreading

- Proofread your writing for spelling, punctuation, and grammar errors.

- Read your piece to an adult.

- Correct and neatly recopy or type your final draft.

- Choose an attention-grabbing title.

Proofreading Symbols

≡	capital letter	Max smith . . .
/	lower-case letter	We like to ᵉEat . . .
⊙	add period	It was fun⊙
?	add question mark	Do you like pizza?
∧	insert, add this	Ten ᵖᵉᵒᵖˡᵉ were coming . . .
ℓ	delete, take out	Jump all around . . .
⌄	add apostrophe	The bike was Sarah's.
❥ ❥	add quotation marks	Jonathon yelled, Supper!
¶	new paragraph	happy. The boy . . .

Teacher Tips for Editing

- Students may gain more understanding if some selections are corrected with the class as a group before requiring students to make corrections independently.

- If using a transparency, use brightly colored markers for clarity.

- Count skill mistakes and give this number to the students to motivate and guide them.

- When using selections for individual work, allow students to edit and revise in colored pencil or pen.

Teacher Tips for Encouraging Young Writers

- Provide students with several ideas and options for their writing.

- Encourage students to write their rough drafts without concern about spelling. Corrections in spelling will come during proofreading.

- Have students share their rough drafts with a buddy or a small group to get suggestions for revisions.

- Provide red pencils or colored pens for children to use while proofreading for spelling and grammar errors.

- Hold individual conferences to read and discuss written work.

- If students have written the rough copy, allow them to type the final draft if possible.

- Encourage children to illustrate their stories. Very young children may want to illustrate before they write, while others will be ready to write before illustrating.

- Children love to share their final products. Staple stories and illustrations into a book and let children read to other students or classrooms.

- Publish stories in a class book to be shared in your reading area. You may want to place a copy in the school library.

- Maintain individual portfolios, including samples of student work.

✎ Skill Lessons
1. Use capital letters correctly.
2. Use correct punctuation.

Anne Frank

anne frank was born on june 12, 1929 in frankfurt, germany she died in a concentration camp in march of 1945 when she caught typhus she was not yet 16 years old. You would agree she was a beautiful girl.

the frank family lived in Germany at the time of hitler's rule adolf hitler believed in developing a superior German race he wanted to eliminate certain groups of people such as the jews the franks and some of the other persecuted jews fled germany to find safety in the city of amsterdam in the netherlands

eventually, even amsterdam was invaded by the German army. the frank family was forced into hiding in the small, upstairs quarters of an office building anne and her family remained in hiding for more than two years they were extremely brave and daring.

during this time, anne recorded her daily activities and personal thoughts in a diary after anne died, her diary was found and published for people everywhere to read anne frank, who dreamed of being a professional writer, was one of the best authors in the world

Suggested Revision
• Cross out the opinions in the article. Replace them with factual sentences.

Name _____

✎ **Skill Lessons**
1. Indicate where paragraphs begin.
2. Use proper punctuation.
3. Use proper capitalization.

Carlos

carlos is a slob he's a nice likeable kid but everything about him is messy his school locker could be mistaken for a toxic-waste site and his mother declared his bedroom a danger zone carlos is a slob in every way one morning carlos did not come to the table for breakfast his mom called for him but he did not answer she knocked on his bedroom door when there was no response she began to worry it was not like carlos to miss breakfast she stood at the door wondering what she should do carlos had to be in there somewhere she yelled his name once again then she decided she must enter the *danger zone* and look for her son

Suggested Revisions
- Write a more interesting title for the story.
- Add a paragraph telling what Carlos's mom saw when she entered the *danger zone*.

✎ Skill Lessons
1. Use correct capitalization and punctuation.
2. Correct the spelling of commonly confused words.
3. Eliminate redundant adjectives.

Jake and His Dad

Deer hunting with his dad was one of Jake's favorite things in the whole wide big world even when he was just a little teeny tiny kid, his father would take him out in the woods and teach him everything he needed to know to be a great wonderful hunter one day

Sitting up camp was something Jake had helped his father do since he was only three years old the big huge canvas tent became their bedroom in the snowy woods, and the cookstove became their kitchen by the time they had the campsite already, the campsite felt almost like home

It was in the woods that Jake had learned how to use a compass and mark a trail "A good hunter doesn't get lost," his father had told him when they had decided on the perfect magnificent hunting spot, they would set motionless for hours, hoping that a deer would wander passed them although Jake was

Continued on page 11.

Jake and His Dad *(cont.)*

too young to shoot, he would watch his father raise his bow and arrow and pull the string back Jake would hold his breath as his father released the string and would watch the arrow fly directly to its target his dad was a skilled talented hunter, and Jake wanted to be just like him

When Jake was finely old mature enough to carry his own bow, his father took him to a special hunting spot Jake had completed the hunters' safety course at school, and he was ready to make his father proud of him "I will bring home a deer. You can count on it," Jake said with quiet confidence

Suggested Revision
• Continue the story. Use descriptive words to tell what happens on Jake's first hunt.

Skill Lessons
1. Add *-ly* to form the adverbs correctly.
2. Write the correct verb tense.

Snorkeling

Tammy and her family excited board the large sailboat with many other vacationers wishing to spend a day snorkeling. As usual, it was a warm morning on the island of Maui. The sun glistening on the ocean waters as the boat left the slip and headed for Molokai, the favored snorkeling spot. Tammy sits next to her father near the stern of the boat. The salty ocean waters spraying over the side of the boat and onto her legs. Soon the sails were up and the snorkelers were sailed effortless to their destination.

Some of the crew passed out snorkeling gear and cheerful give instructions to the passengers. The mask felt tight, and Tammy disliked the rubbery taste of the mouthpiece. Since she was determining to enjoy her first snorkeling experience, she adjusted her gear and practices breathing.

Continued on page 13.

Snorkeling (cont.)

Before too long, Tammy could feel the boat slowing as the crew steered it near the reef and put down the anchors. Tammy watches as some of the other passengers jump bold into the clear, blue water. She decided to ease herself in, using the ladder.

The ocean water was surprising warm and inviting. Tammy tightened her mask and gentle pressed her face into the water. A whole new world appeared before her eyes. Fluorescent-colored fish of various sizes gliding about in the shallow waters. They swam graceful in and out of the reef like underwater performers in a careful choreographed show. Tammy could hardly believe her eyes.

Suggested Revisions
- Write a conclusion for this story. Use plenty of descriptive words to tell about Tammy's experience. Include several adverbs.
- Give the story a more interesting title.

✎ Skill Lessons

1. Use correct subject-verb agreement.
2. Cross out sentences that do not belong.

A Team Victory

Waiting for the gun to fire, the runners of the relay teams kneel at the starting blocks. At the sound of the gunshot, the runners flies out of the blocks and races down the track. They are all wearing shorts. In a flash, each runner reaches forward to pass the baton to the second runner making up his team. How many runners are on a track team? With hearts pounding and muscles aching, the runners presses forward and then carefully passes the baton to the third runner. Several minutes later, another baton exchange are made. The spectators jumps to their feet and explodes with cheers as the fourth runner crosses the line, securing a victory for his whole team!

Suggested Revision

• Replace the overused word *runner* with appropriate synonyms.

✎ Skill Lessons

1. Correct sentence fragments.
2. Correct run-on sentences.
3. Use *a* and *an* correctly.

Water Park

On an hot sunny day in August. Gena's family arrived at the water park dressed in their swimsuits they were expecting to have an great time. Huge water slides and exciting raft rides. In every direction, Gena could see kids laughing, splashing, and having fun. Gena didn't know where to begin and she wanted to do everything all at once.

Gena decided her first ride would have to be the highest, fastest, and wettest ride. In the entire park. She looked around again then, she saw it. Straight ahead, nearly reaching the sky, was the Triple Twister and Gena could tell this was going to be a awesome day!

Suggested Revisions

• Give the story an interesting title.
• Add several descriptive sentences about the park telling what Gena saw and heard.

✏ Skill Lessons

1. Write the titles of books correctly.
2. Use the correct homophones.
3. Eliminate double negatives.
4. Capitalize proper nouns.

A Book Report

James and the Giant Peach is the tail of a young boy who learns that good friends and a bit of courage can improve even life's worst circumstances.

james henry trotter was an orphan forced to live with his too mean ants, aunt sponge and aunt spiker. The aunts were lazy and selfish. They didn't do nothing kind for james. When james was finished with his long list of chores, he was locked away in his room without no friends, no toys, or no delicious things to eat. james was very lonely and unhappy.

One day, james heard a rustling in the leaves and discovered a tiny old man carrying a little sack. The little old man gave the sack to james and told him it would change his life forever. james ran toward the house with the sack, but he slipped, and the sack burst open as it hit the ground. Thousands of little green things wriggled into the earth beneath a peach tree. james new that he had no hope for happiness no more.

Continued on page 17.

A Book Report *(cont.)*

The next day, james was surprised to sea a peach growing on the old, lifeless tree. The peach continued to grow so big it touched the ground. Swarms of people came to see the huge peach. aunt sponge and aunt spiker charged admission and planned to get rich.

james discovered a large whole in the side of the peach. He crawled inside. Once inside the pit, he found a roomful of enormous insects waiting for him. Full of passengers, the peach rolled rapidly down a hill. Moments later, a big splash told them they had landed in the ocean. james and his friends were about to begin a marvelous adventure together.

"James and the Giant Peach" is one of roald dahl's most exciting and popular stories. It has even been made into a motion picture. Other good books by roald dahl include The BFG and "Charlie and the Chocolate Factory." roald dahl has written many other strange yet wonderful stories that shouldn't be missed.

Suggested Revisions
- Change some words that have been used too frequently.
- Write a new, more exciting title.

✎ Skill Lessons

1. Correct the run-on sentences.
2. Correct the sentence fragments.

Whales

Whales are not fish they are mammals. They are warm-blooded animals. They breathe air. They breathe through a blow-hole in the top of their heads. They must come to the water's surface to get air they nurse their babies.

There are two major groups of whales. Toothed whales. Baleen whales. Toothed whales have teeth and eat fish, squid, or cuttlefish.

Instead of teeth, baleen whales have hundreds of thin plates in their mouths. Called baleen or whalebone. The baleen whales catch tiny aquatic organisms each time they fill their mouths with water they eat a lot of krill this way. Two types of baleen whales are the blue whale and the humpback whale.

For centuries. Whales have been hunted and killed, mainly for their blubber. The blubber is used for oil. Today, whale hunting is restricted because whale species are disappearing.

Suggested Revisions

- Rewrite the first paragraph, varying the sentence structure.
- Write a new, more interesting title.

✎ Skill Lessons

1. Remove sentences that do not belong.
2. Use correct pronouns.
3. Use the correct homonyms: *too, to,* and *two.*

Autumn

Autumn is a nice time of year in Michigan. Some people like to go water skiing in the summer. Most people enjoy the changes autumn brings. New sounds, sights, and smells arrive with the crisp wind that replaces the soft summer air.

Early in the season, many people like two pick apples and make good apple pies. They is the time of year for enjoying apple cider, donuts, and hayrides. Pumpkin pies make delicious desserts on Thanksgiving Day.

As the temperatures outside drop, so do the pretty leaves on the trees. Families work together raking they into piles. Children can be heard laughing as he jump into big piles of leaves. Later, the smell of burning leaves often fills the autumn air.

As the autumn air grows even cooler, tree branches begin too look bare under a gray sky. November winds soon whisk away the fallen dried leaves. Michigan says farewell two gentle autumn and hello too the harsh winter that lies ahead.

Suggested Revisions

- Replace the following words with more interesting synonyms:
  nice, people, good, pretty, jump, big, says
- Write a new, more interesting title.

✎ **Skill Lessons**
1. Use *a* and *an* correctly.
2. Use capital letters correctly.

Genius

albert einstein was born in 1879 in ulm, germany. He was three years old before he could talk. When albert was five years old, his father gave him an compass. This sparked his curiosity. he was fascinated with the needle that pointed in the same direction no matter how he moved the compass.

In school, Albert was very interested in algebra and geometry. He disliked the rest of school, but he continued to study until he earned a Ph.D. he could not find a job as an teacher. He took an job as a patent examiner. in his free time he studied physics. He published three papers in that field by the age of 26. They dealt with his theories of relativity and light, as well as other theories of physics. other important scientists recognized the genius of albert einstein. he won the nobel peace prize in 1921 for his work on the photoelectric effect.

einstein, the pacifist, moved from Nazi germany to the u.s. and became a citizen. in 1955, einstein, the genius, died.

Suggested Revision
• Combine related sentences to eliminate the "choppy" sentences.

✎ Skill Lessons

1. Add the appropriate punctuation and capitals.
2. Correct inappropriate language of the business letter.

A Business Letter

152 lucy drive

Fort Worth tx 76156

march 29 1998

washington convention center

900 9th st. NW

Washington, D.C. 20001-4426

To whom It May concern:

Our civics class has been studying the history of our Constitution and the current role of lawmakers in our country. I'm required to present a report on Washington d c. The report must include information about the white house, the capitol, the smithsonian institute, and the famous monuments and memorials. Please send me any brochures and stuff you have on these subjects.

It'll be cool learning about our nation's capital. thank you for your help in this matter.

Yours Truly

Jamie Patterson

Suggested Extension

• Address an envelope in which this letter could be mailed.

✎ Skill Lessons

1. Draw a line through the redundant sentences.
2. Identify where each paragraph should begin.
3. Replace the italicized verbs with more interesting ones.

Ladybugs

Another name for a ladybug is *lady beetle*. It is a beetle. Ladybugs are small insects measuring 10 mm or less in length. A ladybug is a small insect. Ladybugs have six legs. There are more than 4,000 species of ladybugs. Ladybugs are usually red with black spots, but they may also be orange or yellow. Not all ladybugs are red. Like other insects in the beetle family, ladybugs *have* three body parts. They also have two antennae. During the winter, many ladybugs hibernate under leaves, under stones, or in piles of debris. They *get* together and sleep until spring *comes back*. Most beetles are pests to farmers, but ladybugs are quite helpful because of their eating habits. Both adults and larvae *eat* aphids and other plant pests. Some farmers purchase a bag of ladybugs and release them in their fields. The ladybugs feast until the aphids are gone. The ladybugs eat a lot of aphids.

Suggested Revisions

• Write a more creative title for this article.
• Rewrite several sentences to avoid overusing *are* and *is*.

✎ Skill Lessons
1. Use correct verbs.
2. Correct spelling errors.

Pyramids

Nearly five thousand years ago, some of the world's largest stone buildings are created. These are the pyramids of Egypt. They are also some of the largest buildings in the world. What makes them amazing is that the pyramids were builded without machinery or iron tools.

Building the pyramids must have been difficult and dangerous. It was hard work. The heavy limestone blocks used to build the pyramids has to be cut with copper chisels and saws and then moves without cranes and bulldozers. It must have taken thousandes of men many years to build these huge structures.

About 35 major pyramids still stand in Egypt today. Built to protect the bodies of Egyptian kings, the pyramids contain secret passages, hidden rooms, and ramps. Buried with each king were treasures of gold and other precious objectes. Unfortunately, most of the pyramids have been rob of their treasureses. Still, people from around the world travel to visit these fascinating ancient creations today.

Suggested Revision
• Combine or remove sentences to eliminate redundancy in this article.

✎ Skill Lessons

1. Correctly use the comparative and superlative forms of adjectives.
2. Use correct subject-verb agreement.
3. Capitalize proper nouns.

Coral Reefs

Underwater gardens known as coral reefs provides homes to many brightly colored sea creatures. The reefs grow in colorful displays of orange, yellow, green, and purple in warm, shallow waters of seas around the world.

Coral are formed by millions of tiny sea animals called *polyps*. The polyps lives in colonies. Polyps uses the calcium carbonate in the sea water to form a limestone attachment to other polyps. The limestone hardens, and when the animal dies, it leaves a limestone "skeleton." As new polyps attach to these limestone skeletons, the reef grow more larger and larger.

Coral reefs grow in clear shallow ocean waters that are more warmer than 64°F. The world's most largest barrier reef are located off the northeastern coast of australia. It is called the great barrier reef. It is about 1,250 miles long. About 400 different species of polyps form the coral on this reef.

Continued on page 25.

Name _____

Coral Reefs *(cont.)*

Today, many of the world's coral reefs is in danger. Parts of the reefs have been damaged by certain species of starfish which feed on living polyps. Overfishing has disrupted the delicate balance of the reefs' food chain. Tourist boats pollute the water with gasoline and oil. Sewage and poisons from factories pollutes the waters and destroys the coral. Divers have vandalized the beautiful reefs by stepping on them or breaking off pieces to keep as souvenirs.

Suggested Revision
• Write a concluding sentence or paragraph to end the article on a positive note.

✎ Skill Lessons

1. Combine words to make contractions where possible.
2. Draw a line through sentences that do not belong.
3. Correct punctuation errors at the ends of the sentences.

After School

The school bell rang, and the sixth-grade students raced out of the giant front doors of Lincoln Middle School. As Blake ran down the front steps, he threw his jacket and backpack over his shoulder! It was a perfect October day. Blake dashed down the sidewalk through the carpet of fallen leaves. Hearing the crunch of leaves under his feet reminded Blake of the promise he had made.

Each year since Blake's grandfather died, Blake had raked the leaves in his grandmother's yard. Just last week he had promised to rake them again, and today he would keep that promise! Blake loved his grandfather and missed him very much. Blake turned and ran across the field that stretched between the middle school and his grandmother's old farmhouse. Although the grasses were thick and tall, Blake did not feel tired? Running track had strengthened his legs, making this an easy run. As Blake ran toward the north end of the field, he thought about the cold soda and homemade brownies Grandma would have waiting for him.

Continued on page 27.

After School *(cont.)*

Chocolate brownies were his favorite snack, and his grandmother always had a good supply! He liked chewy taffy candy too.

Suddenly, something lying in the grass ahead caught Blake's eye and stopped his thoughts of after-school snacks. Sometimes he made a peanut butter and honey sandwich when he came home from school. Blake slowed his pace; his eyes searched for the object. He wasn't wearing his sunglasses. "What is it?" he wondered? The wind blew slightly and Blake could see it was paper— *green* paper. "Money!" he thought. Blake reached out and grabbed the rumpled green paper. He could not believe his eyes. He had found a $100 bill.

Suggested Revisions
- Complete the story. Tell what Blake does with the money.
  Be sure to use descriptive words and interesting verbs.
- Write an interesting title for the story.

✎ Skill Lessons
1. Make sure all pronouns and their antecedents agree.
2. Correct run-on sentences.

Penguins Keeping Warm

Penguins are unusual birds found in Antarctica and other southern locations. They spend a lot of time in the icy ocean waters, they do not get cold. They are covered with short, thick feathers that help to keep them warm. Plus, beneath his skin, penguins have a layer of blubber. These thick layers of fat keep the penguins warm in icy water.

Baby penguins, called chicks, do not have as much insulation as its parents have they do not yet have blubber or waterproof feathers to keep it warm and dry. The chicks' fluffy down feathers plus their parents' body heat keep it safe from the cold. A small penguin may huddle under the warm body of an adult, and sometimes the adults form a tight circle around a group of several chicks and eventually the little penguins will be able to survive on his own.

Suggested Revision
• Complete the article by adding a final paragraph.

✎ Skill Lessons

1. Correctly use the comparative and superlative forms of adjectives.
2. Use the correct spellings of homophones.

Eagles

One of the most majestic and most powerfulest birds in the world is the eagle. There are about sixty species of eagles, and eagles live on every continent in the world accept for Antarctica.

Eagles are dangerous predators. Eagles use their powerful, sharp talons to capture their pray. The eagle's hooked beak is more strong enough to tear the flesh of the animals it hunts. Some eagles, such as the bald eagle, also scavenge animals that are already dead.

Eagles have the amazing ability to sore on the wind for more longer periods of thyme than other large birds. Eagles have very more sharp eyesight. The eagle's excellent vision allows it to sea even very small pray, such as mice or rabbits, from long distances.

The bald eagle and the golden eagle make their homes in North America. Eagles build they're nests in large trees or on high cliffs. Today, both of these eagles are protected from hunters by the American government.

Suggested Revisions
- Eliminate the over-use of the word *eagle*.
- Rewrite sentences that sound awkward.

✎ **Skill Lessons**
1. Add the proper punctuation to each quotation.
2. Add commas in a series.

Sledding

Look at the snow shouted Judah. It must be a foot deep

Judah and his brother, Michael, planned to race each other down

the big hill located behind the farm. The boys dressed themselves

in their warmest winter clothes pulled on their tall winter boots

grabbed their sleds and rushed outside. Large, white snowflakes

dropped from the sky, instantly covering their knit caps scarves

and mittens. The January air was cold and crisp, and the snow

crunched beneath their feet as the boys charged through the field

toward the hill they called Snow Mountain.

I'll race you to the top of the hill called Judah.

Yeah! And I'll beat you to the bottom laughed Michael. They

sped up the hill together while slipping laughing and shouting.

Suggested Revision
• Continue the dialogue in the story by adding speech from each of
  the boys. Remember to add quotation marks and the other
  necessary punctuation.

Name _____

✎ Skill Lessons
1. Begin each sentence with a capital letter.
2. Number the sentences of each paragraph in logical order.

Christmastime

it is a time to celebrate with family and friends. different families have their own Christmastime traditions. although Christmas day is on the 25th of December, the Christmas season begins right after Thanksgiving and lasts through New Year's Day. christmas is a special time of year.

colored lights are placed on branches of an evergreen. many people top their trees with an angel, while others prefer a star. one Christmas tradition is the decorating of a Christmas tree. ornaments and other decorations are added to the tree as well.

when they awaken, the boys and girls are delighted to find presents from Santa under the Christmas tree. on Christmas Eve, Santa drives his sleigh to deliver gifts to homes around the world. many young children around the world believe in Santa Claus. the youngsters believe that Santa and his elves make toys for all good little boys and girls.

Suggested Revision
• Continue the article. Tell about your favorite tradition of the holiday season.

Name _____

✎ **Skill Lessons**
1. Add quotation marks where necessary.
2. Correct run-on sentences by forming compound sentences.
3. Use correct subject-verb agreement.

Why Fish Have Fins

A long, long time ago, the fish of the sea floated rather than swam. Life in the big sea was simple and pleasant. It was a good life for the fish they was remarkably happy.

Then one day, a new and upsetting law were made by the monster of the deep. All fish will go to school! he hollered.

Schools of fish! That is absurd! Why do we needs to go to school? the fish complained.

Early the next morning, the fish went to school just as they had been ordered floating there was a slow process. When they finally arrived, the teacher were waiting impatiently, flapping his gills and swishing his tail. You are ALL tardy, he blurted. Tomorrow you will be on time or you will be turned into a fish dinner.

The frightened little fish floated down to the store to look for a solution to their problem. The fish tried on some fish fins and each purchased a pair. The fins helped them move through the water more swiftly. Ever since, fish has traveled in schools with special fins made just for them only the fish that are late for school ends up in a fish dinner.

Suggested Revision
• Develop the paragraph about the monster of the deep.

✎ Skill Lessons

1. Make sure all pronouns and their antecedents agree.
2. Correct spelling errors.

A Real Gem!

One of nature's baeutiful gems, the pearl, develops underwater inside the shell of an oyster. A pearl begins to form when a grain of sand or other foriegn matter enters the shell and irritates the mollusk. The mollusk protects itselves by gradually coating the irritant with layers of *nacre*. Nacre is the lustrous lining of the mollusk's shell. This layering process takes several years. Over time, the tiny grane of sand becomes a pearl.

Natural pearls are gathered by pearl divers. Although the divers gather thouzands of oysters, only a handful of pearls are actually harvested. *Cultured* pearls are real pearls that are produced with human help. A grain of sand is plased in an oyster which is carefully monitored for about three years. Then the pearl is harvested. Abowt two oysters in every 100 produces a valuable pearl.

Pearls are most valuable when they are perfectly round and have no blemeshes. Jewelers carefully sort pearls to make jewelry. It look for pearls that are the same size, color, and luster.

Suggested Revision

• Add a final paragraph to finish the article. Include an opinion.

✎ Skill Lessons

1. Write the contractions correctly.
2. Spell out all numbers under 10 and use numerals for those 10 and over.
3. Add apostrophes to possessive nouns.

The Birthday Gift

At last it was Joes birthday. Joe had been waiting all year to turn thirteen. Being twelve was okay. It was sure better than being 8 or nine. Joe was eager to be thirteen and to finally be a teenager. For weeks now, Joes parents had been asking him what present he wanted when he turned thirteen. There was only one thing Joe wanted, only one thing that would make his birthday perfect—an iguana.

Joes parents were'nt thrilled with the idea of having a scaly reptile living in the house, but Joe was persistent in asking. He promised to keep the iguanas cage clean and to keep the iguana in his bedroom at all times. "I do'nt know, Joey," his mother began, "Iguanas are just so ... so creepy. I dont think I could stand it if I saw a little green iguana running loose."

On the morning of his birthday, Joe raced down the hall toward the kitchen. "Happy birthday, Joe," his father greeted him. "Why dont you sit down and enjoy the pancakes your mother

Continued on page 35.

The Birthday Gift *(cont.)*

made for your birthday." Joe ate, but he kept thinking about his birthday present.

"Here, Joey, open your gift," his mother urged as she handed him a box wrapped in red and black paper. Joe looked at the box. It did'nt look like a box that would hold a living creature the size of an iguana. Slowly, he ripped the paper from the box and lifted the lid. A pang of disappointment ran through his body as he stared at the new hockey jersey inside the box.

"Ah, thanks," he began. "Its a really cool shirt. Ill wear it tomorrow." His parents continued smiling. Joe was relieved that they had'nt noticed how disappointed he was with the shirt. "Well, Id better go to school now. Thanks for the special breakfast. And thanks for the shirt, too."

Joe opened the back door, started to step out, and stopped. There on the back step Joe saw a glass aquarium holding a green lizard with a crest of scales on its back. "An iguana!" Joe shouted. Joe turned and looked at his parents who were still smiling. "Thank you! This is the best birthday gift Ive ever gotten!"

Suggested Revision
• Each paragraph contains an overused word. Replace it with other words as needed to make the paragraph sound better.

✎ Skill Lessons
1. Use the correct form for a friendly letter.
2. Add commas and periods where necessary.
3. Correct the use of *good, well, bad,* and *badly.*

Camp Experience

June 1 1999

Dear Mom and Dad

   I am having a well time at camp Each cabin has room for twelve campers and I am getting to know all of my roommates good No one seems to be homesick yet not even me.

   Yesterday we went canoeing down the river. Today it rained so we stayed inside and did arts and crafts. Tomorrow if we don't behave bad we are going hiking in the mountains.

   Camp food doesn't taste as badly as I thought it would. The ice cream is the best Camp is a lot of fun.

Love

Chris

Suggested Revision
• Add adjectives and adverbs to create vivid descriptions.

✎ Skill Lessons

1. Add words to correct the incomplete sentences.
2. Combine sentences to improve the sentence flow.
3. Number the sentences to arrange them in a logical order.

Sundae Treat

Making an ice-cream sundae can be a lot of fun. A delicious experience. Then you will need a serving dish large enough to hold your ice-cream creation. You will also need an ice-cream scoop for scooping the ice cream into bowls. Finally, you are ready to make your sundae. First, you will need to buy all of your favorite ice-cream sundae ingredients.

Finally, use a long-handled spoon to eat your treat and enjoy every single sweet bite. First, put the ice cream in the dish. Use the ice-cream scoop. Three scoops is a good number. Some people like bananas. Pour your favorite toppings over the ice-cream. Caramel, hot fudge, strawberry, or all three. Whipped cream tastes good over. Small candy pieces. Place a cherry on top of the whipped cream. Add any other ingredients to your sundae that you like.

Suggested Revision

• Many of the sentences in the first paragraph begin the same way. Create a more interesting paragraph by changing the word order and eliminating overused words.

Skill Lessons
1. Change abbreviated words into their unabbreviated form.
2. Add commas where needed.
3. Cross out sentences that reflect the author's opinion rather than factual information.

Geysers

The word geyser comes from an Icelandic word which means "to gush." It is a funny word. Geysers are found in three locations in the world. In Iceland, there are dozens of geysers in a 10-mi. site of barren lava fields. In New Zealand, geysers are found in a fertile green area—a very different environment. Yellowstone Natl. Pk. in the western U.S. has at least 200 active geysers.

A geyser is a hot spring that shoots boiling water and steam into the air. Geysers are found where water drains deep beneath the earth's surface. Water seeps down channels to rocks that are very hot. The water is then heated by the rocks. The hot water then turns to steam and forces its way out of the channel along with the water above it. The water forms a steamy column above the earth's surface. It is an awesome sight! After an eruption some of the water seeps back into the channel and the process is repeated all over again. When the water becomes very hot the geyser will erupt again.

Continued on page 39.

Geysers *(cont.)*

Yellowstone Natl. Pk. is located in the state of Wyo. The land in the park was created by volcanic eruptions over 60,000 yrs. ago. The molten rock beneath the surface provides the heat for the geysers. Old Faithful is one of the geysers in Yellowstone Pk. It throws hot water and steam about 120–150 ft. into the air every 76 min. Old Faithful earned its name from its predictable schedule. It has been erupting regularly for over 80 yrs. It is the most beautiful geyser in the park.

All geysers act differently. Some may erupt several times in an hr. Others may not erupt for mos. Some geysers are not predictable at all. Some geysers soar high like Old Faithful while others merely bubble above the ground. Geysers are fascinating to study.

Suggested Revision
• Rewrite the sentences that reflect opinions so that they state factual information instead.

✎ Skill Lessons

1. Add quotation marks where necessary.
2. Correct spelling errors.
3. Correct capitalization errors.
4. Add apostrophes to contractions.

The Haircut

Just a trim. Thats what my mother said. My mother gave me $10.00 and droped me off at Lou's barber shop. I didnt want to go. I protested, telling her my hair was the perfect length. Besides, I needed it a little longer to keep my head warm in the winter. Mom smiled and said, tell Lou you only want a trim ill be back in half an hour.

Ive known Lou since i was just a little kid. He always seemed like a pretty decent guy. Last year he sponsored our Baseball Team. We wore candy-red tee shirts with big black letters that said "Lou's Barber Shop—A Cut Above the Rest." he came to all the games and even gave the guys free haircuts.

I walked into the shop and saw Lou cutting mr. garcia's hair. He said he was almost finished and told me to hop up in the

Continued on page 41.

The Haircut *(cont.)*

other chair. A few minutes later, Lou came over with the scissors and electric trimmers in his hands. I told him I only want a trim becuase my hair is the perfect length and just rite for keeping my head warm.

He nodded and began to trim and trim and trim some more. the next thing I knew, my hair was "trimmed" almost completely away. My ears were cold and my forehead was much bigger than I remembered it. Didnt he no what a trim was? Either Lou was going def or he was still angry about all those baseball games we lost!

Suggested Revisions
• Add discussion between the narrator and Lou, the barber.
• Write a more interesting title.

✏ Skill Lessons

1. Improve wordy sentences by crossing through any unnecessary words.
2. Rewrite the underlined sentences to make them concise.

Tasmania

This article is about the island of Tasmania that is an island state of Australia located 150 miles off the mainland. Tasmania and its islands are a little smaller than the state of Maine. <u>Hobart is a city that is located on the southeast coast of the island, and it is Tasmania's capital.</u> Tasmania has a cool, wet climate. <u>There are many eucalyptus forests on the island of Tasmania which are home to many animals.</u>

It is interesting to know that Tasmania is home to the black marsupial, the Tasmanian devil. It gets its name from its appearance. The Tasmanian devil is about the size of a small dog. Its diet may consist of other small animals, such as opossums, snakes, lizards, rabbits, wallabies, and birds. It hunts for its food at night. I also want to say that in spite of their fierce reputations, Tasmanian devils are shy and will usually run away from people.

Suggested Revisions

• Write a more interesting title for the article.
• Add a third paragraph that includes your opinion.

Answer Key

Anne Frank

Skill Lessons
1. Use capital letters correctly.
2. Use correct punctuation.

Anne frank was born on june 12, 1929 in frankfurt, germany. she died in a concentration camp in march of 1945 when she caught typhus. she was not yet 16 years old. You would agree she was a beautiful girl.

the frank family lived in Germany at the time of hitler's rule. adolf hitler believed in developing a superior German race. he wanted to eliminate certain groups of people such as the jews. the franks and some of the other persecuted jews fled germany to find safety in the city of amsterdam in the netherlands.

eventually, even amsterdam was invaded by the German army. the frank family was forced into hiding in the small, upstairs quarters of an office building. anne and her family remained in hiding for more than two years. they were extremely brave and daring.

during this time, anne recorded her daily activities and personal thoughts in a diary. after anne died, her diary was found and published for people everywhere to read. anne frank, who dreamed of being a professional writer, was one of the best authors in the world.

Page 8

Carlos

Skill Lessons
1. Indicate where paragraphs begin.
2. Use proper punctuation.
3. Use proper capitalization.

Carlos is a slob. he's a nice, likeable kid, but everything about him is messy. his school locker could be mistaken for a toxic-waste site, and his mother declared his bedroom a danger zone. carlos is a slob in every way. one morning carlos did not come to the table for breakfast. his mom called for him, but he did not answer. she knocked on his bedroom door. when there was no response, she began to worry. it was not like carlos to miss breakfast. she stood at the door wondering what she should do. carlos had to be in there somewhere. she yelled his name once again. then she decided she must enter the *danger zone* and look for her son.

Page 9

Jake and His Dad

Skill Lessons
1. Use correct capitalization and punctuation.
2. Correct the spelling of commonly confused words.
3. Eliminate redundant adjectives.

Deer hunting with his dad was one of Jake's favorite things in the whole wide big world, even when he was just a little teeny tiny kid, his father would take him out in the woods and teach him everything he needed to know to be a great wonderful hunter one day.

Setting up camp was something Jake had helped his father do since he was only three years old. the big huge canvas tent became their bedroom in the snowy woods, and the cookstove became their kitchen. by the time they had the campsite all ready already, the campsite felt almost like home.

It was in the woods that Jake had learned how to use a compass and mark a trail. "A good hunter doesn't get lost," his father had told him when they had decided on the perfect magnificent hunting spot, they would sit set motionless for hours, hoping that a deer would wander past them although Jake was

Page 10 *Continued on page 11.*

Jake and His Dad (cont.)

too young to shoot, he would watch his father raise his bow and arrow and pull the string back. Jake would hold his breath as his father released the string and would watch the arrow fly directly to its target. his dad was a skilled talented hunter, and Jake wanted to be just like him.

When Jake was finely finally old mature enough to carry his own bow, his father took him to a special hunting spot. Jake had completed the hunters' safety course at school, and he was ready to make his father proud of him. "I will bring home a deer. You can count on it," Jake said with quiet confidence.

Page 11

Snorkeling

Skill Lessons
1. Add -ly to form the adverbs correctly.
2. Write the correct verb tense.

Tammy and her family excited boarded the large sailboat with many other vacationers wishing to spend a day snorkeling. As usual, it was a warm morning on the island of Maui. The sun glistened on the ocean waters as the boat left the slip and sat headed for Molokai, the favored snorkeling spot. Tammy sat next to her father near the stern of the boat. The salty ocean waters sprayed over the side of the boat and onto her legs. Soon the sails were up and the snorkelers were sailing effortlessly to their destination.

Some of the crew passed out snorkeling gear and cheerfully gave instructions to the passengers. The mask felt tight, and Tammy disliked the rubbery taste of the mouthpiece. Since she was determined to enjoy her first snorkeling experience, she adjusted her gear and practiced breathing.

Continued on page 13.

Page 12

© Instructional Fair • TS Denison 43 IF5145 *Skills for Young Writers*

Page 15

✏ **Skill Lessons**
1. Correct sentence fragments.
2. Correct run-on sentences.
3. Use a and an correctly.

Water Park

On an hot sunny day in August, Gena's family arrived at the water park dressed in their swimsuits, they were expecting to have an great time. Huge water slides and exciting raft rides. In every direction, Gena could see kids laughing, splashing, and having fun. Gena didn't know where to begin, she wanted to do everything all at once.

Gena decided her first ride would have to be the highest, fastest, and wettest ride, in the entire park. She looked around again, then, she saw it. Straight ahead, nearly reaching the sky, was the Triple Twister. Gena could tell this was going to be an awesome day!

Page 18

✏ **Skill Lessons**
1. Correct the run-on sentences
2. Correct the sentence fragments.

Whales

Whales are not fish, they are mammals. They are warm-blooded animals. They breathe air. They breathe through a blow-hole in the top of their heads. They must come to the water's surface to get air, they nurse their babies.

There are two major groups of whales, toothed whales, baleen whales. Toothed whales have teeth and eat fish, squid, or cuttlefish.

Instead of teeth, baleen whales have hundreds of thin plates in their mouths, called baleen or whalebone. The baleen whales catch tiny aquatic organisms each time they fill their mouths with water, they eat a lot of krill this way. Two types of baleen whales are the blue whale and the humpback whale.

For centuries, whales have been hunted and killed, mainly for their blubber. The blubber is used for oil. Today, whale hunting is restricted because whale species are disappearing.

Page 14

✏ **Skill Lessons**
1. Use correct subject-verb agreement.
2. Cross out sentences that do not belong.

A Team Victory

Waiting for the gun to fire, the runners of the relay teams kneel at the starting blocks. At the sound of the gunshot, the runners race out of the blocks and races down the track. They are all wearing shorts. In a flash, each runner reaches forward to pass the baton to the second runner making up his team. Many runners are on a track team. With hearts pounding and muscles aching, the runners press forward and then carefully pass the baton to the third runner. Several minutes later, another baton exchange are made. The spectators jump to their feet and explode with cheers as the fourth runner crosses the line, securing a victory for his whole team!

Page 17

A Book Report (cont.)

The next day, james was surprised to see a peach growing on the old, lifeless tree. The peach continued to grow so big it touched the ground. Swarms of people came to see the huge peach, aunt sponge and aunt spiker charged admission and planned to get rich.

james discovered a large hole in the side of the peach. He crawled inside. Once inside the pit, he found a roomful of enormous insects waiting for him. Full of passengers, the peach rolled rapidly down a hill. Moments later, a big splash told them they had landed in the ocean. james and his friends were about to begin a marvelous adventure together.

James and the Giant Peach is one of roald dahl's most exciting and popular stories. It has even been made into a motion picture. Other good books by roald dahl include The BFG and Charlie and the Chocolate Factory. roald dahl has written many other strange yet wonderful stories that shouldn't be missed.

Page 13

Snorkeling (cont.)

Before too long, Tammy could feel the boat slowing as the crew steered it near the reef and put down the anchors. Tammy watched as some of the other passengers jumped boldly into the clear, blue water. She decided to ease herself in, using the ladder.

The ocean water was surprisingly warm and inviting. Tammy tightened her mask and gently pressed her face into the water. A whole new world appeared before her eyes. Fluorescent-colored fish of various sizes glided about in the shallow waters. They swam gracefully in and out of the reef like underwater performers in a carefully choreographed show. Tammy could hardly believe her eyes.

Page 16

✏ **Skill Lessons**
1. Write the titles of books correctly.
2. Use the correct homophones.
3. Eliminate double negatives.
4. Capitalize proper nouns.

A Book Report

James and the Giant Peach is the tale of a young boy who learns that good friends and a bit of courage can improve even life's worst circumstances.

james henry trotter was an orphan forced to live with his two aunts, mean aunt sponge and aunt spiker. The aunts were lazy and selfish. They didn't do anything kind for james. When james was finished with his long list of chores, he was locked away in his room without any friends, any toys, or any delicious things to eat. james was very lonely and unhappy.

One day, james heard a rustling in the leaves and discovered a tiny old man carrying a little sack. The little old man gave the sack to james and told him it would change his life forever. james ran toward the house with the sack, but he slipped, and the sack burst open as it hit the ground. Thousands of little green things wriggled into the earth beneath a peach tree. james knew that he had no hope for happiness anymore.

Continued on page 17.

A Business Letter (Page 21)

✏ **Skill Lessons**
1. Add the appropriate punctuation and capitals.
2. Correct inappropriate language of the business letter.

152 lucy drive
Fort Worth, tx 76156
march 29, 1998

washington convention center
900 9th st. NW
Washington, D.C. 20001-4426

To whom It May concern:

Our civics class has been studying the history of our Constitution and the current role of lawmakers in our country. I'm required to present a report on Washington, D.C. The report must include information about the white house, the capitol, the smithsonian institute, and the famous monuments and memorials. Please send me any brochures and other information you have on these subjects.

It'll be confirming interesting to learn about our nation's capital. thank you for your help in this matter.

Yours, truly,

Jamie Patterson

Page 21

Coral Reefs (Page 24)

✏ **Skill Lessons**
1. Correctly use the comparative and superlative forms of adjectives.
2. Use correct subject-verb agreement.
3. Capitalize proper nouns.

Underwater gardens known as coral reefs provide homes to many brightly colored sea creatures. The reefs grow in colorful displays of orange, yellow, green, and purple in warm, shallow waters of seas around the world.

Coral are formed by millions of tiny sea animals called *polyps.* The polyps live in colonies. Polyps use the calcium carbonate in the sea water to form a limestone attachment to other polyps. The limestone hardens, and when the animal dies, it leaves a limestone "skeleton." As new polyps attach to these limestone skeletons, the reef grows larger and larger.

Coral reefs grow in clear, shallow ocean waters that are more warmer than 64°F. The world's largest barrier reef is located off the northeastern coast of australia. It is about 1,250 miles long. About 400 different species of polyps form the coral on this reef.

Continued on page 25.

Page 24

Genius (Page 20)

✏ **Skill Lessons**
1. Use *a* and *an* correctly.
2. Use capital letters correctly.

albert einstein was born in 1879 in ulm, germany. He was three years old before he could talk. When albert was five years old, his father gave him a compass. This sparked his curiosity. he was fascinated with the needle that pointed in the same direction no matter how he moved the compass.

In school, Albert was very interested in algebra and geometry. He disliked the rest of school, but he continued to study until he earned a Ph.D. he could not find a job as a teacher. He took a job as a patent examiner. in his free time he studied physics. He published three papers in that field by the age of 26. They dealt with his theories of relativity and light, as well as other theories of physics. other important scientists recognized the genius of albert einstein. he won the nobel peace prize in 1921 for his work on the photoelectric effect.

einstein, the pacifist, moved from Nazi germany to the u.s. and became a citizen. in 1955, einstein, the genius, died.

Page 20

Pyramids (Page 23)

✏ **Skill Lessons**
1. Use correct verbs.
2. Correct spelling errors.

Nearly five thousand years ago, some of the world's largest stone buildings were created. These are the pyramids of Egypt. They are also some of the largest buildings in the world. What makes them amazing is that the pyramids were built without machinery or iron tools.

Building the pyramids must have been difficult and dangerous. It was hard work. The heavy limestone blocks used to build the pyramids had to be cut with copper chisels and saws and then moved without cranes and bulldozers. It must have taken thousands of men many years to build these huge structures.

About 35 major pyramids still stand in Egypt today. Built to protect the bodies of Egyptian kings, the pyramids contain secret passages, hidden rooms, and ramps. Buried with each king were objects treasures of gold and other precious objects. Unfortunately, most of the pyramids have been robbed of their treasures. Still, people from around the world travel to visit these fascinating ancient creations today.

Page 23

Autumn (Page 19)

✏ **Skill Lessons**
1. Remove sentences that do not belong.
2. Use correct pronouns.
3. Use the correct homonyms: *too, to,* and *two.*

Autumn is a nice time of year in Michigan. Some people like to go swimming in the summer. Most people enjoy the changes autumn brings. New sounds, sights, and smells arrive with the crisp wind that replaces the soft summer air.

Early in the season, many people like to pick apples and make good apple pies. This is the time of year for enjoying apple cider, donuts, and hayrides. Pumpkin pies make delicious desserts on Thanksgiving Day.

As the temperatures outside drop, so do the pretty leaves on the trees. Families work together raking them into piles. Children can be heard laughing as they jump into big piles of leaves. Later, the smell of burning leaves often fills the autumn air.

As the autumn air grows even cooler, tree branches begin too look bare under a gray sky. November winds soon whisk away the fallen dried leaves. Michigan says farewell to gentle autumn and hello too the harsh winter that lies ahead.

Page 19

Ladybugs (Page 22)

✏ **Skill Lessons**
1. Draw a line through the redundant sentences.
2. Identify where each paragraph should begin.
3. Replace the italicized verbs with more interesting ones.

Answers will vary.

Another name for a ladybug is *lady beetle.* It is a beetle. Ladybugs are small insects measuring 10 mm or less in length. A ladybug is a small insect. Ladybugs have six legs. There are more than 4,000 species of ladybugs. Ladybugs are usually red with black spots, but they may also be orange or yellow. Not all ladybugs are red. Like other insects in the beetle family, ladybugs have three body parts. They also have two antennae. During the winter, many ladybugs hibernate under leaves, under stones, or in piles of debris. They get together and sleep until spring comes back. Most beetles are pests to farmers, but ladybugs are quite helpful because of their eating habits. Both adults and larvae eat aphids and other plant pests. Some farmers purchase a bag of ladybugs and release them in their fields. The ladybugs feast until the aphids are gone. The ladybugs eat a lot of aphids.

Page 22

After School (cont.)

Chocolate brownies were his favorite snack, and his grandmother always had a good supply. ~~He liked chewy taffy candy too.~~

Suddenly, something lying in the grass ahead caught Blake's eye and stopped his thoughts of after-school snacks. ~~Sometimes he made a peanut butter and honey sandwich when he came home from school.~~ Blake slowed his pace; his eyes searched for the object. ~~He wasn't wearing his sunglasses.~~ "What is it?" he wondered. The wind blew slightly and Blake could see it was paper—green paper. "Money!" he thought. Blake reached out and grabbed the rumpled green paper. He could not [couldn't] believe his eyes.

He had found a $100 bill.

Continued on page 27.

Skill Lessons
1. Combine words to make contractions where possible.
2. Draw a line through sentences that do not belong.
3. Correct punctuation errors at the ends of the sentences.

After School

The school bell rang, and the sixth-grade students raced out of the giant front doors of Lincoln Middle School. As Blake ran down the front steps, he threw his jacket and backpack over his shoulder. It was a perfect October day. Blake dashed down the sidewalk through the carpet of fallen leaves. Hearing the crunch of leaves under his feet reminded Blake of the promise he'd made.

Each year since Blake's grandfather died, Blake had raked [raked] the leaves in his grandmother's yard. Just last week he had promised to rake them again, and today he would [he'd] keep that promise. Blake ~~loved his grandfather and missed him very much.~~ Blake turned and ran across the field that stretched between the middle school and his grandmother's old farmhouse. Although the grasses were thick and tall, Blake did not feel tired [didn't] Running track had strengthened his legs, making this an easy run. As Blake ran toward the north end of the field, he thought about the cold soda and homemade brownies Grandma would have waiting for him.

Page 26

Sledding

"Look at the snow!" shouted Judah. "It must be a foot deep!" Judah and his brother, Michael, planned to race each other down the big hill located behind the farm. The boys dressed themselves in their warmest winter clothes, pulled on their tall winter boots, grabbed their sleds, and rushed outside. Large, white snowflakes dropped from the sky, instantly covering their knit caps, scarves, and mittens. The January air was cold and crisp, and the snow crunched beneath their feet as the boys charged through the field toward the hill they called Snow Mountain.

"I'll race you to the top of the hill," called Judah.

"Yeah! And I'll beat you to the bottom," laughed Michael. They sped up the hill together while slipping, laughing, and shouting.

Page 30

Skill Lessons
1. Add the proper punctuation to each quotation.
2. Add commas in a series.

Coral Reefs (cont.)

Today, many of the world's coral reefs is [are] in danger. Parts of the reefs have been damaged by certain species of starfish which feed on living polyps. Overfishing has disrupted the delicate balance of the reefs' food chain. Tourist boats pollute the water with gasoline and oil. Sewage and poisons from factories pollutes [pollute] the waters and destroys [destroy] the coral. Divers have vandalized the beautiful reefs by stepping on them or breaking off pieces to keep as souvenirs.

Page 25

Skill Lessons
1. Make sure all pronouns and their antecedents agree.
2. Correct run-on sentences.

Penguins Keeping Warm

Penguins are unusual birds found in Antarctica and other southern locations. They spend a lot of time in the icy ocean waters, they [yet] do not get cold. They are covered with short, thick feathers that help to keep them warm. Plus, beneath his [their] skin, penguins have a layer of blubber. These thick layers of fat keep the penguins warm in icy water.

Baby penguins, called chicks, do not have as much insulation as its [their] parents have, they [them] do not yet have blubber or waterproof feathers to keep it [them] warm and dry. The chicks' fluffy down feathers plus their parents' body heat keep it [them] safe from the cold. A small penguin may huddle under the warm body of an adult, and [and] sometimes the adults form a tight circle around a group of several chicks, and [and] eventually the little penguins will be able to survive on his [their] own.

Page 28

Skill Lessons
1. Correctly use the comparative and superlative forms of adjectives.
2. Use the correct spellings of homophones.

Eagles

One of the most majestic and most powerfuler [powerful] birds in the world is the eagle. There are about sixty species of eagles, and eagles live on every continent in the world accept [except] for Antarctica.

Eagles are dangerous predators. Eagles use their powerful, sharp talons to capture their pray [prey]. The eagle's hooked beak is mea [meat] strong enough to tear the flesh of the animals it hunts. Some eagles, such as the bald eagle, also scavenge animals that are already dead.

Eagles have the amazing ability to sore [soar] on the wind for more longer periods of thyme [time] than other large birds. Eagles have very mere [more] sharp eyesight. The eagle's excellent vision allows it to sea [see] even very small pray [prey], such as mice or rabbits, from long distances.

The bald eagle and the golden eagle make their homes in North America. Eagles build they're [their] nests in large trees or on high cliffs. Today, both of these eagles are protected from hunters by the American government.

Page 29

Skill Lessons
1. Make sure all pronouns and their antecedents agree.
2. Correct spelling errors.

A Real Gem!

beautiful

One of nature's ~~beautiful~~ gems, the pearl, develops underwater inside the shell of an oyster. A pearl begins to form when a grain of sand or other ~~foreign~~ matter enters the shell and irritates the mollusk. The mollusk protects ~~itselfs~~ itself by gradually coating the irritant with layers of nacre. Nacre is the lustrous lining of the mollusk's shell. This layering process takes several years. Over time, the tiny ~~grane~~ grain of sand becomes a pearl.

thousands

Natural pearls are gathered by pearl divers. Although the divers gather ~~thousands~~ of oysters, only a handful of pearls are actually harvested. Cultured pearls are real pearls that are produced with human help. A grain of sand is ~~plased~~ placed in an oyster which is carefully monitored for about three years. Then the pearl is harvested. ~~Abowt~~ About two oysters in every 100 produces a valuable pearl.

blemishes

Pearls are most valuable when they are perfectly round and have no ~~blemeshes~~. Jewelers carefully sort pearls to make jewelry.

They

~~I~~ look for pearls that are the same size, color, and luster.

Camp Experience

Skill Lessons
1. Use the correct form for a friendly letter.
2. Add commas and periods where necessary.
3. Correct the use of good, well, bad, and badly.

June 1999

Dear Mom and Dad,

good

I am having a ~~well~~ time at camp. Each cabin has room for twelve campers and I am getting to know all of my roommates

well

~~good~~. No one seems to be homesick yet, not even me.

Yesterday we went canoeing down the river. Today it rained, so we stayed inside and did arts and crafts. Tomorrow if we

badly

don't behave ~~bad~~ we are going hiking in the mountains.

bad

Camp food doesn't taste as ~~badly~~ as I thought it would.

The ice cream is the best. Camp is a lot of fun.

Love,

Chris

Skill Lessons
1. Add quotation marks where necessary.
2. Correct run-on sentences by forming compound sentences.
3. Use correct subject-verb agreement.

Why Fish Have Fins

A long, long time ago, the fish of the sea floated rather than swam. Life in the big sea was simple and pleasant. It was a good life for the fish, they ~~was~~ were remarkably happy.

and were

Then one day, a new and upsetting law ~~were~~ made by the monster of the deep. All fish will go to school! he hollered.

need

Schools of fish! That is absurd! Why do we ~~need~~ to go to school? the fish complained.

Early the next morning, the fish went to school just as they had been ordered. Floating there was a slow process. When they finally arrived, the teacher ~~were~~ waiting impatiently, flapping

was

his gills and swishing his tail. You are ALL tardy, he blurted.

have

Tomorrow you will be on time or you will be turned into a fish dinner.

The frightened little fish floated down to the store to look for a solution to their problem. The fish tried on some fish fins and each purchased a pair. The fins helped them move through the water more swiftly. Ever since, fish ~~has~~ traveled in schools with special fins made just for them. Only the fish that are late for

end

school ~~end~~ up in a fish dinner.

The Birthday Gift (cont.)

made for your birthday, Joe ate, but he kept thinking about his birthday present.

"Here, Joey, open your gift," his mother urged as she handed him a box wrapped in red and black paper. Joe looked at the box.

didn't

It ~~didn't~~ look like a box that would hold a living creature the size of an iguana. Slowly, he ripped the paper from the box and lifted the lid. A pang of disappointment ran through his body as he stared at the new hockey jersey inside the box.

It's I'll I'll

"Ah, thanks," he began. "~~Its~~ a really cool shirt. ~~Il~~ wear it

hadn't

tomorrow." His parents continued smiling. Joe was relieved that they ~~hadn't~~ noticed how disappointed he was with the shirt.

I'd

"Well, ~~Id~~ better go to school now. Thanks for the special breakfast. And thanks for the shirt, too."

Joe opened the back door, started to step out, and stopped. There on the back step Joe saw a glass aquarium holding a green lizard with a crest of scales on its back. "An iguana!" Joe shouted. Joe turned and looked at his parents who were still smiling.

I've

"Thank you! This is the best birthday gift ~~Ive~~ ever gotten!"

Skill Lessons
1. Begin each sentence with a capital letter.
2. Number the sentences of each paragraph in logical order.

Christmastime

(2) It is a time to celebrate with family and friends. (1) Different families have their own Christmastime traditions. Although Christmas day is on the 25th of December, the Christmas season begins right after Thanksgiving and lasts through New Year's Day.

(1) Christmas is a special time of year.

(2) Colored lights are placed on branches of an evergreen. Many people top their trees with an angel, while others prefer a star. (1) One Christmas tradition is the decorating of a Christmas tree. (3) Ornaments and other decorations are added to the tree as well.

(1) When they awaken, the boys and girls are delighted to find presents from Santa under the Christmas tree. (3) On Christmas Eve, Santa drives his sleigh to deliver gifts to homes around the world. (2) Many young children around the world believe in Santa Claus. (4) The youngsters believe that Santa and his elves make toys for all good little boys and girls.

Skill Lessons
1. Write the contractions correctly.
2. Spell out all numbers under 10 and use numerals for those 10 and over.
3. Add apostrophes to possessive nouns.

The Birthday Gift

At last it was Joe's birthday. Joe had been waiting all year to

13

turn ~~thirteen~~. Being ~~twelve~~ was okay. It was sure better than

eight 13

being ~~8~~ or nine. Joe was eager to be ~~thirteen~~ and to finally be a teenager. For weeks now, Joe's parents had been asking him what present he wanted when he turned ~~thirteen~~. There was only one thing Joe wanted, only one thing that would make his birthday perfect—an iguana.

weren't

Joe's parents ~~were not~~ thrilled with the idea of having a scaly reptile living in the house, but Joe was persistent in asking. He promised to keep the iguana's cage clean and to keep the iguana

don't

in his bedroom at all times. "I ~~do not~~ know, Joey," his mother be-

don't

gan. "Iguanas are just so ...so creepy. I ~~do not~~ think I could stand it if I saw a little green iguana running loose."

On the morning of his birthday, Joe raced down the hall toward the kitchen. "Happy birthday, Joe," his father greeted him.

don't

"Why ~~don't~~ you sit down and enjoy the pancakes your mother

Continued on page 35.

Continued on page 39.
Continued on page 41.

Page 39

geysers (cont.)

Yellowstone National Park is located in the state of Wyoming. The land in the park was created by volcanic eruptions over 60,000 years ago. The molten rock beneath the surface provides the heat for the geysers. Old Faithful is one of the geysers in Yellowstone Park. It throws hot water and steam about 120–150 feet into the air every 76 minutes. Old Faithful earned its name from its predictable schedule. It has been erupting regularly for over 80 years. ~~It is the most beautiful geyser in the park.~~

All geysers act differently. Some may erupt several times in hours. Others may not erupt for months. Some geysers are not predictable at all. Some geysers soar high like Old Faithful while others merely bubble above the ground. ~~Geysers are fascinating to study.~~

Page 39

Page 42

✎ **Skill Lessons**
1. Improve wordy sentences by crossing through any unnecessary words.
2. Rewrite the underlined sentences to make them concise.

Tasmania   Answers will vary.

~~This article is about the island of~~ Tasmania ~~that~~ is an island state of Australia located 150 miles off the mainland. Tasmania and its islands are a little smaller than the state of Maine. Hobart ~~is a city that is~~ located on the southeast coast of the island. ~~and~~ ~~There~~ It is Tasmania's capital. Tasmania has a cool, wet climate. The many eucalyptus forests on the island ~~of Tasmania which~~ are home to many animals.

~~It is interesting to know that~~ Tasmania is home to the black marsupial, the Tasmanian devil. It gets its name from its appearance. The Tasmanian devil is about the size of a small dog. Its diet may consist of other small animals, such as opossums, snakes, lizards, rabbits, wallabies, and birds. It hunts for its food at night. ~~I also want to say that~~ in spite of their fierce reputations, Tasmanian devils are shy and will usually run away from people.

Page 42

Page 38

✎ **Skill Lessons**
1. Change abbreviated words into their unabbreviated form.
2. Add commas where needed.
3. Cross out sentences that reflect the author's opinion rather than factual information.

geysers

The word geyser comes from an Icelandic word which means "to gush." ~~It is a funny word.~~ Geysers are found in three locations in the world. In Iceland, there are dozens of geysers in a 10-mile site of barren lava fields. In New Zealand, geysers are found in a fertile green area—a very different environment. Yellowstone National Park in the United States in the western U.S. has at least 200 active geysers.

A geyser is a hot spring that shoots boiling water and steam into the air. Geysers are found where water drains deep beneath the earth's surface. Water seeps down channels to rocks that are very hot. The water is then heated by the rocks. The hot water then turns to steam and forces its way out of the channel along with the water above it. The water forms a steamy column above the earth's surface. ~~It is an awesome sight!~~ After an eruption, some of the water seeps back into the channel and the process is repeated all over again. When the water becomes very hot, the geyser will erupt again.   *Continued on page 39.*

Page 38

Page 41

The Haircut (cont.)

other chair. A few minutes later, Lou came over with the scissors and electric trimmers in his hands. I told him I only want a trim. because my hair is the perfect length and just right for keeping my head warm.

He nodded and began to trim and trim and trim some more. the next thing I knew, my hair was "trimmed" almost completely away. My ears were cold and my forehead was much bigger than I remembered it. Didn't he know what a trim was? Either Lou was going deaf or he was still angry about all those baseball games we lost!

Page 41

Page 37

✎ **Skill Lessons**
1. Add words to correct the incomplete sentences.
2. Combine sentences to improve the sentence flow.
3. Number the sentences to arrange them in a logical order.

Sundae Treat

Making an ice-cream sundae can be a lot of fun and delicious. Then you will need a serving dish large enough to hold your ice-cream creation. You will also need an ice-cream scoop for scooping the ice cream into bowls. Finally, you are ready to make your sundae. First, you will need to buy all of your favorite ice-cream sundae ingredients.

Finally, use a long-handled spoon to eat your treat and enjoy every single sweet bite. First, put three scoops of choice ice cream in the dish. Some people like bananas. Pour your favorite toppings over the ice-cream. ~~Caramel, hot fudge, strawberry, or all three.~~ Whipped cream tastes good over small candy pieces. Place a cherry on top of the whipped cream. Add any other ingredients to your sundae that you like.

Page 37

Page 40

✎ **Skill Lessons**
1. Add quotation marks where necessary.
2. Correct spelling errors.
3. Correct capitalization errors.
4. Add apostrophes to contractions.

The Haircut

Just a trim. That's what my mother said. My mother gave me $10.00 and dropped me off at Lou's barber shop. I didn't want to go. I protested, telling her my hair was the perfect length. Besides, I needed it a little longer to keep my head warm in the winter. Mom smiled and said, tell Lou you only want a trim. I'll be back in half an hour.

I've known Lou since I was just a little kid. He always seemed like a pretty decent guy. Last year he sponsored our baseball team. We wore candy-red tee shirts with big black letters that said "Lou's Barber Shop—A Cut Above the Rest." he came to all the games and even gave the guys free haircuts.

I walked into the shop and saw Lou cutting mr. garcia's hair. He said he was almost finished and told me to hop up in the   *Continued on page 41.*

Page 40
